What on Earth?
Life in the
Wetlands

What on Earth?

Nose like a snorkel!

What uses
its nose like a
snorkel and can
stay underwater
for a long time?

Turn the page for the answer.

First published in 2005 by
Book House an imprint of
The Salariya Book Company
25 Marlborough Place
Brighton
BN1 1UB

HB ISBN 1-905087-43-8
PB ISBN 1-905087-44-6

Visit our website at **www.book-house.co.uk**
for free electronic versions of:
You Wouldn't Want to be an Egyptian Mummy!
You Wouldn't Want to be a Roman Gladiator!
Avoid joining Shackleton's Polar Expedition!
You Wouldn't want to Sail on a 19th-Century Whaling Ship!

Due to the changing nature of internet links, The Salariya Book Company
has developed an online list of websites related to the subject of this book.
This site is updated regularly. Please use this link to access the list:
http://www.book-house.co.uk/WOE/wetlands

A catalogue record for this book is available from the British Library.

Printed and bound in China.

Editor:	Ronald Coleman
Senior Art Editor:	Carolyn Franklin
DTP Designer:	Mark Williams

Picture Credits Julian Baker: 8, 9(t), 17, Mark Bergin: 4,
10, 20-21(c), 21(t) Elizabeth Branch: 1, 2, 8(b), 9, 22, 23(t),
Roger Hutchins: 4-5(b), 6-7, 11, Daniel Heuclin, NHPA: 12,
Mirko Stelzner, NHPA: 13, Christopher Ratier, NHPA: 14,
William Paton, NHPA: 15, Hellio and Van Ingen, NHPA: 20,
Martin Wendler, NHPA: 24, Stephen Dalton, NHPA: 25,
Paal Hermansen, NHPA: 26, PhotoDisc: 3, 16, 27, 28, 29,
Digital Vision: 18(b), 23(b), Corbis: 18(r), 19, John Foxx: 31

snifffffff!
snifffffff!

What on Earth?

A tapir!
The tapir also uses its nose to
sniff out plants and to grab
the leaves it wants to eat.

What on Earth? Life in the Wetlands

CAROLYN SCRACE

BOOK HOUSE

Can a terrapin bark?

Go to page 22 for the answer!

Contents

What on Earth?

Clever stickleback!

The male three-spined stickleback, builds a nest from bits of underwater plants.

Introduction

Wetlands are not just muddy swamps or murky bogs! They are packed full of amazing plants and animals. Many of these would die without the food, water and shelter that wetlands provide. Wetlands can be large or small and they can be hot or cold!

Are there different types of wetland?

Swamps, bogs, fens and marshes are the main types of wetland. Where they are found in the world and the types of soil and weather they have are what make them all look very different.

Are wetlands always wet?

No, some wetlands are always wet but others dry up during hot times of the year. A wetland only has shallow, slow-moving water, it is never deep or fast-flowing like a river or sea.

What is happening above the water?

Turn the page for the answer!

What are wetlands?

Seas and oceans are not wetlands! Large lakes and rivers are not wetlands! A wetland is an area of land that is wet for some, or all of the year. Wetlands can be formed if it rains a lot and the water doesn't drain away. Snow that melts and rivers that overflow can also make a wetland.

Look at this picture of an African swamp

This African swamp is in the middle of a desert and is the only place where these plants and animals can find water. See how many plants and animals you can spot.

Knobthorn acacia

Sitatunga

African pygmy goose

African jacana

Spoonbill

Leopard tortoise

Purple heron

Pirate butterfly

Pond skater

Anopheles mosquito

African pike

Tiger fish

Jewelled cichlid

Black-striped rana frog

Where are wetlands?

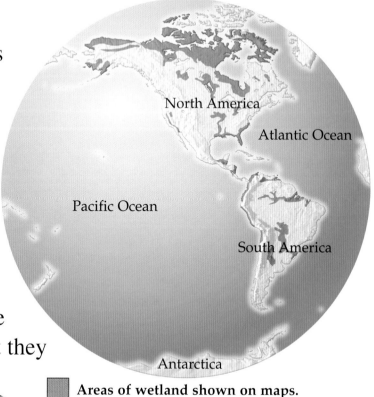

There are wetlands on every continent in the world except for **chilly** Antarctica. Antarctica is ice-covered. Because there is no soil there for water to soak into, there are no wetlands. The Arctic, northern Canada and Russia are nearly as cold as Antarctica but they do have wetland areas.

North America

Atlantic Ocean

Pacific Ocean

South America

Antarctica

Areas of wetland shown on maps.

Can you grow rice in a wetland?

Surinam toad

Yes. In India there are many wetlands and nearly three quarters of these are used for growing rice. China has the largest wetland in Asia! And in Europe, Asia and parts of North America there are even more wetlands.

Where is the World's largest wetland?

The largest wetland is in Brazil, South America. It is enormous - four times the size of the Florida Everglades in North America!

Which continent has most wetlands?

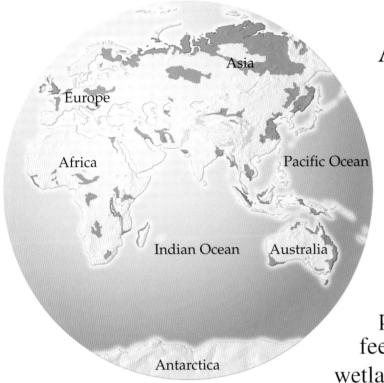

Asia

Europe

Africa

Pacific Ocean

Indian Ocean

Australia

Antarctica

Africa has more wetlands than any other continent. For a few months each year there is a lot of rain in Africa and the water collects in the wetland areas. During the rest of the year there is little or no rain. Without water, grasses and plants die so the animals that feed off them move to wetland areas for food.

Do people live in wetlands?

Yes. People all over the world have adapted to living in wetlands.

What on earth is this strange bird?

This weird wetland bird is called the **whale-headed stork** from Africa. It has a massive hooked bill which it uses for finding fish in the muddy waters!

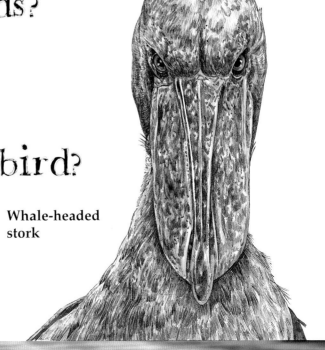

Whale-headed stork

What is a wetland food-chain?

When plants die in or around a wetland, their leaves **sink** to the bottom of the water. The dead leaves are eaten by insects that live in the water, and by pond snails and tiny fish. These creatures are then eaten by larger fish or frogs, newts and birds. This is called a food-chain!

What is plankton?

The smallest plants and animals in the water are called plankton. Some of the plankton are too small to see! A dragonfly nymph lives in the bottom of a reed swamp. It eats tadpoles and small insects that feed on plankton. The dragonfly nymph grows into an adult dragonfly that eats other, larger insects. The dragonfly is then eaten by a hungry bird, a spider or even a frog!

What eats a frog?

A great diving beetle floats to the surface of the water to breathe. It stores air in special tubes in its body. Then it dives down into the water to eat tadpoles, pond snails and even small fish. Great diving beetles are then eaten by frogs. So what eats a frog? Some snakes, birds and lizards like to eat frogs!

Great diving beetle

Tadpole

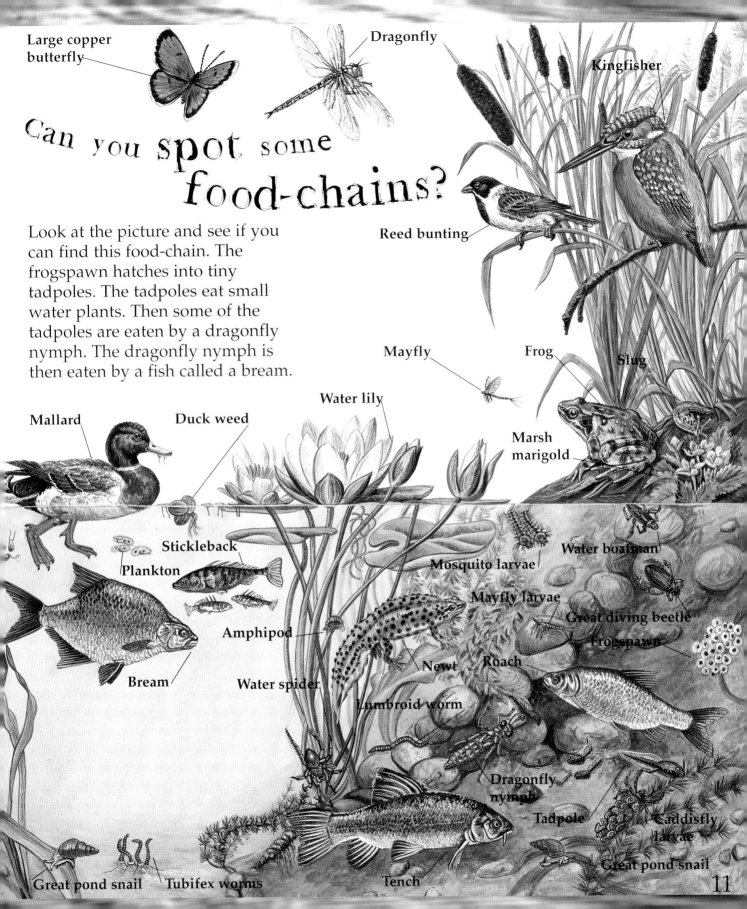

Large copper butterfly

Dragonfly

Kingfisher

Can you spot some food-chains?

Reed bunting

Look at the picture and see if you can find this food-chain. The frogspawn hatches into tiny tadpoles. The tadpoles eat small water plants. Then some of the tadpoles are eaten by a dragonfly nymph. The dragonfly nymph is then eaten by a fish called a bream.

Mayfly

Frog

Slug

Water lily

Mallard

Duck weed

Marsh marigold

Stickleback

Plankton

Mosquito larvae

Water boatman

Mayfly larvae

Great diving beetle

Amphipod

Newt

Roach

Frogspawn

Bream

Water spider

Lumbroid worm

Dragonfly nymph

Tadpole

Caddisfly larvae

Great pond snail

Tubifex worms

Tench

Great pond snail

11

Are wetlands all the same?

Swamps, bogs, marshes and fens are all different types of wetland. Swamps can be found in fresh water and in salty sea water in hot or cold areas of the world. Bogs are only found in colder climates and are different from swamps. A thick dark material called peat lines the bottom of a bog. Its surface is often completely covered by a green 'carpet' of moss.

steamy mangrove swamp!

Mangrove trees grow in hot, salt-water swamps. The mangrove trees (below), have special roots that grow out of their trunks and branches. These roots hold the trees firmly in the muddy soil and supply them with food and oxygen.

What on Earth?

Almost no oxygen?

Swamp mud contains almost no oxygen. This is why the roots of mangrove trees grow above the mud - to absorb oxygen.

What are marshes and fens?

Marshes and fens are types of wetland. Most of the year their soil is either waterlogged or under water. However, they may dry up completely during a very hot summer. Salt marshes are found near the sea. The grasses and plants that grow in these marshes can live in salt-water and can cope with the different levels of sea water caused by tides.

A salt-water marsh (below) in Africa. An Elephant cools down in the muddy water.

Muddy water!

What is green all over?

A fen. Fens have green moss growing on them and marshes have none. Also, fens are usually wetter or flooded longer than marshes.

What on Earth? Do marshes stink?

Yes. Some marshes really do stink. When wetland plants die they rot, and the process of rotting makes marsh gas that is really stinky!

What plants are in wetlands?

Each type of wetland suits a different sort of plant. Plants are very important as they add oxygen to the water. Many of the plants found in wetlands have **adapted** special ways to live in wet conditions. There are three types of plant that live there. Some, like reeds grow out of the water, others like water lilies float on top of the water. Some plants live completely under the water.

What on Earth?

As big as a water lily !

The largest water lily grows in the Amazon River basin in South America. It can be the size of a big round kitchen table!

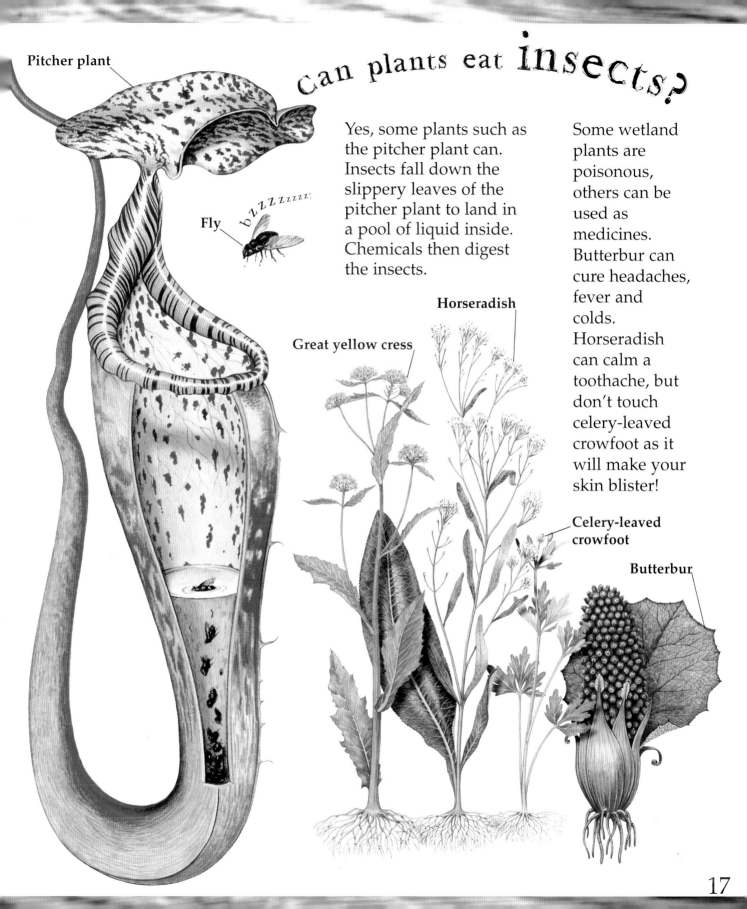

Pitcher plant

Can plants eat insects?

Fly

bzzzzzzz!

Yes, some plants such as the pitcher plant can. Insects fall down the slippery leaves of the pitcher plant to land in a pool of liquid inside. Chemicals then digest the insects.

Some wetland plants are poisonous, others can be used as medicines. Butterbur can cure headaches, fever and colds. Horseradish can calm a toothache, but don't touch celery-leaved crowfoot as it will make your skin blister!

Horseradish

Great yellow cress

Celery-leaved crowfoot

Butterbur

What **birds** and **animals** live there?

Many birds and animals live in or near a wetland. Some of them have special feet to stop them **sinking** in the wet mud. Both the sitatunga (see page 7) and reindeer, have toes that spread apart as they walk on swampy wetland. Can birds walk on water? Yes, the jacana (see page 6), has feet with long thin toes that help it to walk on floating leaves!

The godwit is a wading bird. Wading birds have long legs and beaks which they use for catching food.

What **sweats** pink goo?

A hippopotamus has pink sweat that keeps it cool! It is the largest animal that lives in swamps. It weighs as much as four cars and can open its mouth wide enough to eat a table. Its tusks can be as long as cricket bats!

Why the long neck?

Herons are another type of wading bird. They wade into shallow water on their long legs. Using their long necks and beaks they reach down into the water to find small crabs and shellfish.

What on Earth?

What makes this amazing journey?

What migrates all the way from chilly wetlands in the Arctic to hot, steamy wetlands in South America?

Small birds like sandpipers and plovers! These tiny birds make this incredible journey in search of food and warmth.

19

Are there any fish?

Fish that live in swampy areas usually have deep, thin bodies to help them to swim easily through the dense vegetation. Most of these fish can live in water where there is little oxygen. Some, like the lung fish can even breathe air. A fish called the mailed catfish uses its stomach to breathe!

Can fish walk?

Yes, mudskippers (below) can skip across mud on their fins faster than you can walk. They can even climb up tree roots!

Pike

Fierce fish?

Pike are fierce fish that are often found in reed swamps. They use their strong jaws to catch their prey which includes ducklings and coots. The pike will stay hidden among the plants until its prey passes and then it darts out and grabs it.

painful pincers?

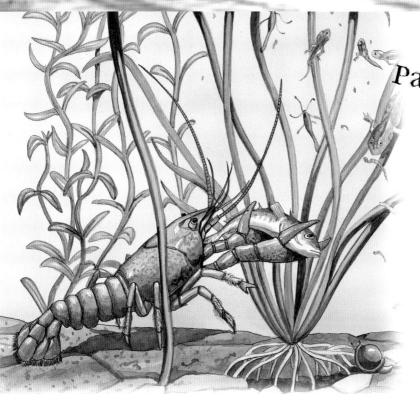

Crayfish are not fish, they are crustaceans related to crabs and lobsters. Crayfish live in lakes, rivers and swamps. They have two large pincers or claws which they use to catch their prey. Crayfish hunt at night and eat snails, small fish and other water animals.

Crayfish

What on Earth?

40-year-old fish?

Yes. Some carp can live for up to 40 years! Carp live in lakes and slow moving rivers. They use four feelers in the corners of their mouth to find food in the muddy water.

Do scary creatures live there?

Crocodiles and alligators live in tropical swamps. Many snakes and turtles live in wetlands, and some of them have special ways of catching food. The mata-mata turtle from South America has a shell that looks like a piece of **dead wood**. Small fish and animals, attracted by the ragged skin around its neck which looks like pieces of food are sucked into the turtle's mouth.

All insects living in swamps are able to breathe air. Some push tubes, like snorkels, out of the water to breathe through.

Woof woof?

Terrapins bark when angry! The painted terrapin lives in ponds, lakes and marshes in North and South America.

What on Earth?

What changes shape and grows legs?

Frogs, toads and salamanders! Most of them start life as legless tadpoles that live in water. As they get bigger they change shape, grow legs and then live on land!

Swordtail

Electric eel

Painted terrapin

Hatchet fish

Silver dollar

Cardinal tetra

Neon tetra

Chocolate cyclid

Mata-mata turtle

What is the World's biggest snake?

The anaconda! A fully grown anaconda can be as long as three cars. It squeezes its prey to death and can take up to a week to digest a large animal!

Dragonfly

Anaconda

Caiman

Crocodile or alligator?

Crocodiles and alligators look very similar. To tell the difference look at their teeth. A crocodile's lower front teeth can be seen when it closes its mouth but an alligator's are hidden!

Why are wetlands so important?

Wetlands help to save the world's coastlines. The roots of wetland plants hold soil in place which stops it being **swept** away by strong ocean waves and currents. Wetlands can prevent flooding. They act like giant sponges, soaking up water and slowing it down. They also filter the water that passes through them making it cleaner.

Wetlands are very important because the survival of many endangered species relies on the water, food and shelter they find there.

The Brazilian tapir is an endangered wetland animal.

What on Earth?

Can wetlands keep the planet clean?

Yes. Wetlands trap many chemicals that pollute our planet. Chemicals such as fertilisers, mercury, lead and bacteria that cause diseases can all be filtered out of the water that passes through a wetland.

Are wetlands under threat?

In the last 100 years, over half of the world's wetlands have disappeared. People have drained them to build roads and cities or turned them into farmland. They have built canals and dams that take water away from wetland areas to supply cities and factories. Wetlands have been destroyed by mining and by logging. Some wetlands have been poisoned when harmful chemicals from factories and farming are left to pour into them. Many countries now protect their wetland areas.

How would you survive in a wetland?

There is plenty of food to be found in a wetland, such as edible berries and plants, fish and shellfish. But do be careful because there are very large snakes and animals that would like to eat **you** instead!

Wetland Dangers

Hippopotamus The best way to stay safe is never to get between a hippopotamus and water!

Alligator Keep well away from an alligator. Don't throw anything at it and never try to feed one!

Anaconda Stay well away from the water. An anaconda is slow to move on land but sure to catch you underwater!

What to take Check-list

Wear **long trousers** tucked into knee-high **wellington boots** to keep your legs dry. Carry a **stick** to test the ground for sogginess, you don't want to sink in the mud! Take a **fishing rod** to catch your dinner and a box of **matches** to light a fire to cook the fish. You will need a **map** to find your way and a **two-way radio** in case you need help! Cover yourself in special **cream** to stop the insects biting you. Do not drink the **water** - bring your own!

What do you know about wetlands?

1 Are wetlands ever deep?

2 Which continent has the most wetlands?

3 What eats a great diving beetle?

4 Why do the roots of the mangrove tree grow above the mud?

5 What happens if you touch celery-leaved crowfoot?

6 Which fish can live for up to forty years?

7 How can you tell the difference between a crocodile and an alligator?

8 Can a terrapin bark?

9 How long does an anaconda take to digest a small animal?

10 Do wetlands keep the planet clean?

Go to page 32 for the answers!

Can you guess
how fast a
hippopotamus
can swim underwater?

Index

Pictures are shown in **bold** type.

Answers

1   No. (See page 5)
2   Africa. (See page 9)
3   Frogs. (See page 10)
4   To absorb oxygen. (See page 13)
5   It will make your skin blister! (See page 17)
6   Carp. (See page 21)
7   Look at their teeth. (See page 23)
8   Yes - if it's angry! (See page 22)
9   Over a week. (See page 23)
10 Yes. (See page 25)

An adult hippopotamus can swim underwater at a speed of 8 km/h (4.9 mph). That is a fast walking pace for a human.